For Hannah and Tommy

First published 1984 by
Walker Books Ltd,
184-192 Drummond Street,
London NW1 3HP

First printed 1984
Printed and bound by
L.E.G.O., Vicenza, Italy

British Library Cataloguing in Publication Data
Oxenbury, Helen
Our dog.–(First picture books)
I. Title II. Series
823'.914[J] PZ7

ISBN 0-7445-0182-2

Our Dog

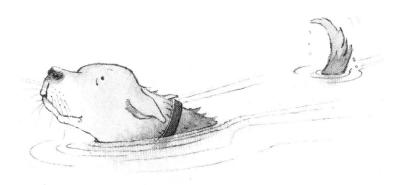

Helen Oxenbury

WALKER BOOKS
LONDON

Our dog has to go for a walk
every day.
She stares at us until we
take her.

One day she found a smelly pond
and jumped into it.
'Poo! You smell disgusting!'
we told her.

Then she rolled in the mud.
'Pretend she's not ours,'
whispered Mum. 'We must get her
home quickly and give her a bath.'

We made her wait
outside the kitchen door.
Mum filled the bath.
'I'll put her in,' Mum said.
'Now hold on tight! Don't
let her jump out!'

'Quick! Where's the towel?'
Mum shouted. 'She'll make
everything wet!'

We chased her out of the
kitchen and down the hall.

She ran up the stairs
and into the bedroom.
We caught her on the bed.
'It's no good!' Mum said.
'We'll just have to take her for
another walk, to dry in the air.'